D0602299

The Science of the Human Body

LIVINGSCIENCE

Lauri Seidlitz

Gareth Stevens Publishing
MILWAUKEE

For a free color catalog describing Gareth Stevens' list of high-quality books and multimedia programs, call 1-800-542-2595 (USA) or 1-800-461-9120 (Canada). Gareth Stevens Publishing's Fax: (414) 225-0377.

Library of Congress Cataloging-in-Publication Data available upon request from publisher. Fax (414) 225-0377 for the attention of the Publishing Records Department.

ISBN 0-8368-2570-5 (lib. bdg.)

This edition first published in 2000 by
Gareth Stevens Publishing
1555 North RiverCenter Drive, Suite 201
Milwaukee, WI 53212 USA

Project Co-ordinator: Meaghan Craven
Series Editor: Linda Weigl
Copy Editors: Marg Cook, Rennay Craats, and Samantha Paterson
Design and Illustration: Warren Clark and Chantelle Sales
Cover Design: Carole Knox
Layout: Lucinda Cage
Gareth Stevens Editor: Rita Reitci

Every reasonable effort has been made to trace ownership and to obtain permission to reprint copyright material. The publishers would be pleased to have any errors or omissions brought to their attention so that they may be corrected in subsequent printings.

Photograph Credits:
Corel Corporation: pages 5, 7 right, 10 right, 13, 16, 17 center, 17 bottom, 17 right, 19 right, 21 left, 24, 26, 28 top; Rennay Craats: page 20 right; Eyewire: pages 14, 18 left, 20 left; Ivy Images: page 11 left; Tom Stack & Associates: pages 8, 9; Photodisc: cover, pages 6, 12, 21 right, 25 left, 29, 30 left, 30 right, 31 center, 31 bottom; Neil Sankoff: pages 11 top, 25 right; Visuals Unlimited: pages 4 (Jeff Greenberg), 7 left (Jeff Greenberg), 10 left (Jeff Greenberg), 11 right (W. Ormerod), 15 (Mark E. Gibson), 17 top (Wally Eberhart), 18 right (David M. Phillips), 19 left (Jeff Greenberg), 22 left (Arthur Gurmankin, Mary Morina), 23 top (Cheyenne Rouse), 23 bottom (Jeff Greenberg), 27 top, 28 bottom (Inga Spence), 30 center (Glenn M. Oliver), 31 top (L. Linkhart); Linda Weigl: pages 22 right, 27 bottom.

Printed in Canada

1 2 3 4 5 6 7 8 9 04 03 02 01 00

Contents

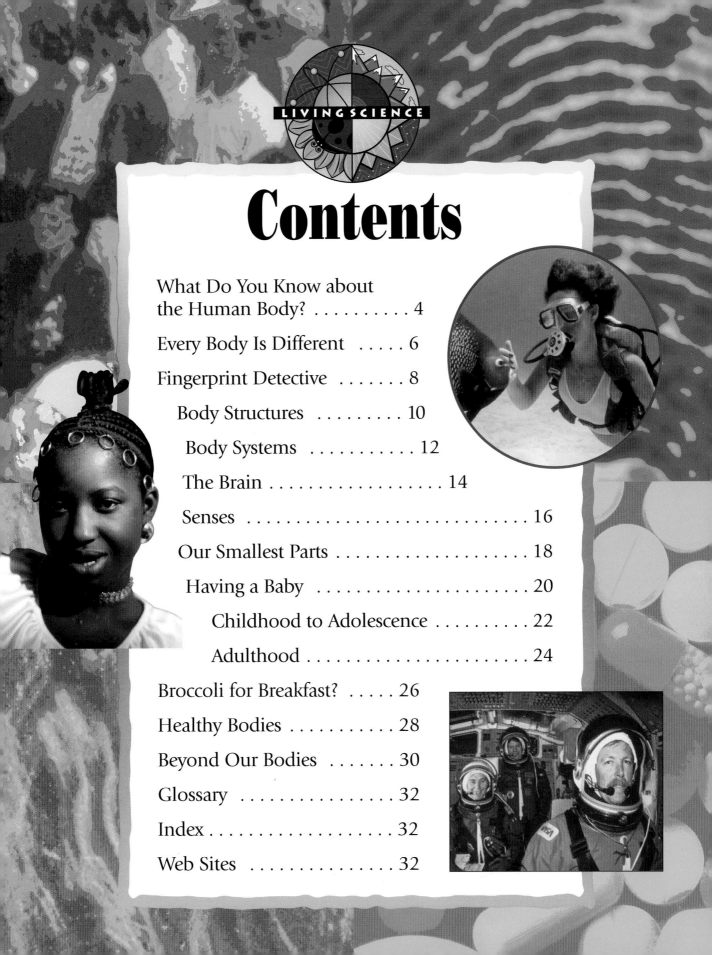

What Do You Know about the Human Body?

You may know more about the human body than you think. After all, you have a body of your own! Your body has many features in common with the people shown on this page. All of you have heads, mouths, legs, and arms. Can you find eight other common features?

Human beings look alike in many ways.

The human body also has many features in common with other animals. Humans belong to a group of animals called mammals. Mammals all have hair or fur, warm blood, and young that drink their mothers' milk. Which other mammal do you think is most like a human? Why?

Activity

Draw Mammals

Draw two mammals you might see in a zoo. How are they alike? How are they different?

How Other Mammals Are Like Humans

Cheetahs	Dogs	Gorillas	Whales
• Cheetah kittens drink milk from their mother.	• Dogs have hair to protect their bodies.	• Gorillas can change the expressions on their faces to communicate.	• Whales breathe air to survive.

How Other Mammals Are Unlike Humans

• Cheetahs can run up to 70 miles (112 kilometers) an hour.

• Dogs walk on four legs.

• Gorillas use their long arms to help them walk.

• Whales have **streamlined** bodies to help them swim in the ocean.

Every Body Is Different

No two people in the world look exactly alike. Hair, skin, and eyes come in different colors. People's bodies are built differently. Their height, width, and weight are not the same. Even chins, lips, and noses have many sizes and shapes.

Twins may seem to be identical, but differences do exist between them.

Body differences make each person one of a kind.

We have many words that describe how people look. Eyes are blue, green, brown, or hazel. Hair is curly, straight, wavy, blond, brown, black, red, gray, thick, stringy, long, or short. Or it may not be there at all! People are tall, short, or of average height. Human skin is smooth, wrinkled, black, pink, red, brown, golden, freckled, pale, or tanned. Bodies are thin, muscular, plump, or somewhere in between.

People from the same families can have similar features because they have the same **ancestors**.

People may look like their parents, grandparents, or other ancestors.

Puzzler

Members of a family often look alike. If the mother has curly hair, and the father has straight hair, what kind of hair might the baby have?

Answer:
This question has more than one right answer. The baby could have straight hair, curly hair, or something in between.

Fingerprint Detective

Every person in the world has a different skin pattern on his or her fingertips. This pattern exists even before we are born, and it never changes. We leave a copy of the pattern on everything we touch. The copy is called a fingerprint.

Fingerprints come in three main patterns: arches, loops, and whorls.

Arches	Loops	Whorls

Fingerprints are easy to see if an object is dusted with powder.

Police use fingerprints to find out who has committed a crime. They sprinkle a special powder on objects at the crime scene. This powder sticks to oily fingerprints and shows their pattern. Detectives compare these fingerprints to the fingerprints of people who might have committed the crime. They try to find a match.

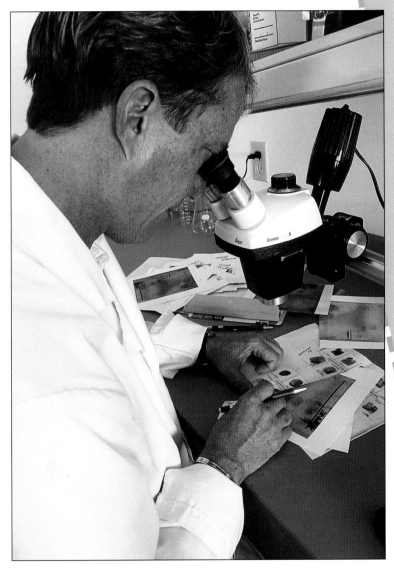

Scientists work in laboratories to prepare fingerprints for identification.

Activity

Solve the Crime

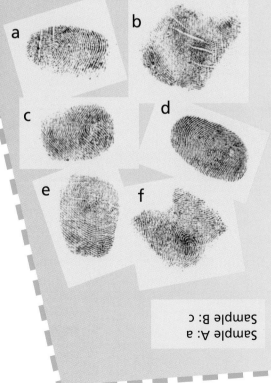

Sample A

Sample B

Detectives found two fingerprints at the scene of a crime. Can you find a match on this page?

a

b

c

d

e

f

Sample A: a
Sample B: c

Body Structures

Structures inside and outside the human body protect it, help it move, and give it shape. Muscles and bones work together inside our bodies. They give our bodies support and strength. Skin, hair, and nails work as a protective outer surface.

Body Structures

Bones and Teeth

- are strong, stiff parts that support the body

- form a frame for the body called a skeleton

- protect the red bone **marrow** that makes new blood cells

Hair and Nails

- are made of dead body cells

- help protect the body and keep it warm

Puzzler

Humans have seven bones in their necks. How many bones do you think a giraffe has in its neck?

Answer: A giraffe has the same number of neck bones as a human. The giraffe's bones are just much bigger!

Skin	Muscles

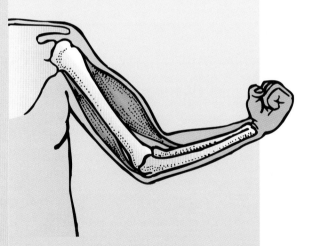

- covers and protects the body

- helps control body temperature

- keeps fluids inside the body

- provides the sense of touch

- can be **involuntary**, like the continually beating heart muscle

- can be **voluntary**, like the arm and leg muscles when you exercise

- pull bones to move different parts of the body

Body Systems

Groups of cells that do special jobs in the body are called organs. Sometimes many organs work together. They form a body system. Important body systems move **nutrients** around the body, and help us breathe, digest food, and get rid of wastes.

Digestion

People use teeth and jaws to chew food so that it is small enough to swallow. The stomach and **intestines** break the food into tiny nutrient pieces. Nutrients then go from the intestines to the blood.

Waste

The body cannot use everything that is eaten. Leftover waste ends up in the **bladder** or **rectum**. It then leaves the body.

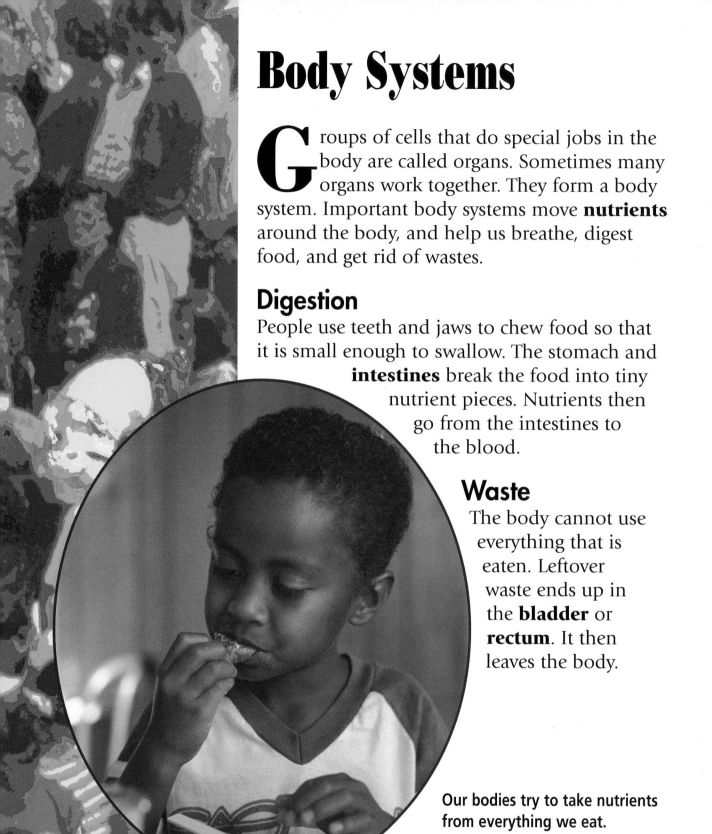

Our bodies try to take nutrients from everything we eat.

The heart is a strong muscle that pumps blood through the body. It beats more than 100,000 times each day.

Circulation

Blood is a liquid. It moves through all parts of the body in a process called circulation. Blood carries nutrients and oxygen to all cells in the body. Cells need nutrients and oxygen to grow, do work, and repair themselves. Blood also carries away waste materials, such as **carbon dioxide**.

Breathing

We need oxygen to live. Lungs send oxygen from air we breathe in to the blood. Blood sends carbon dioxide, a body waste, to the lungs for the body to breathe out.

Activity

Get the Beat

Place two fingers lightly on the inside of your wrist below your thumb. Can you feel the beating? That is your heart beat.

1. Count how many times your heart beats in one minute.
2. Record this number as your resting heart rate.
3. Run around or jump for one minute.
4. Count your heart rate again.
5. What change did you find? How do you think exercise affects the heart?

The Brain

The brain is the most important part of a body system called the **nervous system**. Long, thin cells called nerves connect the brain to all parts of the body. Messages travel along the nerves at speeds of 249 miles (400 kilometers) per hour.

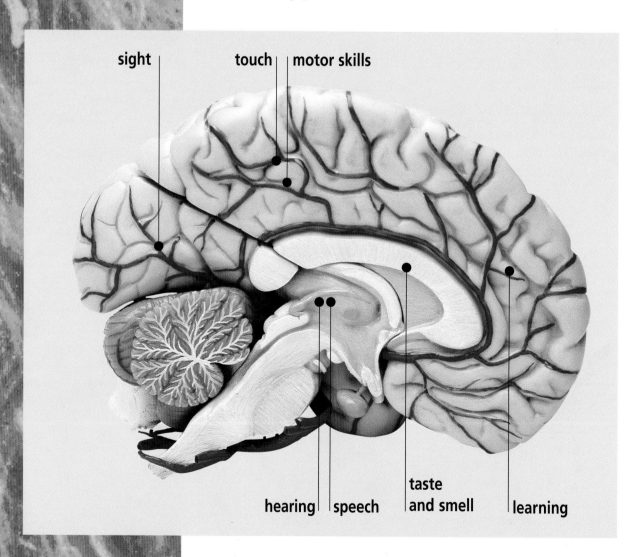

sight · touch · motor skills

hearing · speech · taste and smell · learning

Different parts of the brain control different senses and actions.

The brain is like a computer. It controls everything the body does. The brain tells our heart to speed up or slow down. It controls our breathing. The brain allows us to move, think, learn, and remember. It must be kept safe from harm.

Hard hats and helmets protect the head from injury. What jobs or sports require people to wear head protection?

Puzzler

The brain controls our breathing. It tells the body when to bring in more air. Take a deep breath and hold it for as long as you can. Time yourself. What happens?

Answer:
After about a minute, the brain knows the body needs more oxygen. It then forces you to breathe out used air and breathe in fresh air.

Senses

The tongue, ears, eyes, nose, and skin are sense organs. They send information about the world around us to the brain. The brain tells the body how to react. Do you know which sense belongs to each sense organ?

Sight

The eyes collect light and make a picture signal for the brain. The brain tells the body what it is seeing and how to respond.

Hearing

The outer ears collect sound and send it into the inner ears. The brain interprets the sound and tells us what we are hearing.

Taste

Many tiny bumps called taste buds cover the tongue. Different parts of the tongue sense different tastes.

Touch

Tiny sensors in the skin let the brain know when the body is touching something. The brain tells the body how to react to everything the skin touches.

Smell

The nose detects smells in air and signals the brain. The brain helps identify the smells.

Puzzler

You can often tell which sense an animal uses most. Just look for its biggest sense organ. Which sense is most important to the animals in the photos? Which of your senses is most important to you?

a) Rabbit

b) Lemur

c) Rhino

Answer: a) hearing b) eyesight c) smell

17

Our Smallest Parts

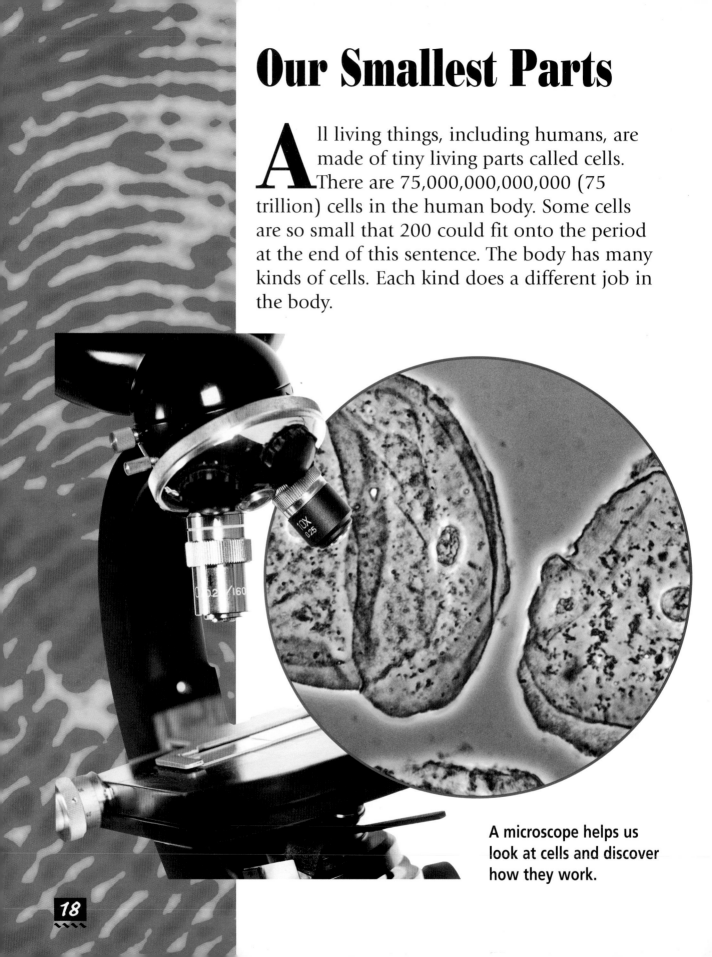

All living things, including humans, are made of tiny living parts called cells. There are 75,000,000,000,000 (75 trillion) cells in the human body. Some cells are so small that 200 could fit onto the period at the end of this sentence. The body has many kinds of cells. Each kind does a different job in the body.

A microscope helps us look at cells and discover how they work.

A human begins to grow when cells from a mother and father combine. These two cells make a new cell that grows into a baby. This is the reason you may look like your mother or father. Your body was made from a tiny part of each of their bodies. Your parents were made from a tiny part of each of their parents.

Sometimes brothers and sisters look alike. Often they look very different! They may look like their mother, their father, or one of their parents' relatives.

Puzzler

All animals begin life as a single cell. The cell contains all the information needed to build a new animal, such as a dog, a bird, or a person. What instructions would a baby bird cell have that a baby human cell would not have?

Answer:
Your answer might include instructions for building a beak, feathers, and wings.

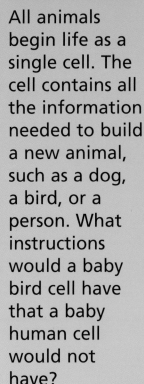

Having a Baby

Human bodies grow very quickly before they are born. They grow in their mothers' bodies during **pregnancy**. Food and oxygen from the mother's body help the baby grow. Nutrients from the mother's blood reach the baby through a tube called the umbilical cord.

A human baby usually grows for nine months before it is ready to be born.

Doctors can take pictures of babies before they are born.

Babies are born with all the parts they will ever have. These body parts grow larger and become more useful. The baby does not grow new parts after birth.

Babies depend on adults for food and protection until they learn how to take care of themselves. Most animals are born knowing how to take care of themselves. This knowledge is called instinct. Humans must learn almost everything from their parents and other adults.

All mammals have belly buttons. This is the spot where the umbilical cord was attached.

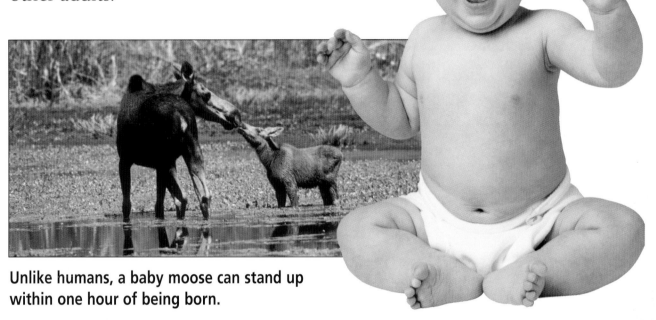

Unlike humans, a baby moose can stand up within one hour of being born.

Puzzler

A mouse grows for 20 days before it is ready to be born. An elephant grows 624 days. A deer grows 215 days. Using this information, figure out how many days a cow needs to grow before it is born.

Answer:
A deer is about the same size as a cow. A good guess would be close to the number of days for a deer. A cow actually grows 281 days before it is ready to be born.

Childhood to Adolescence

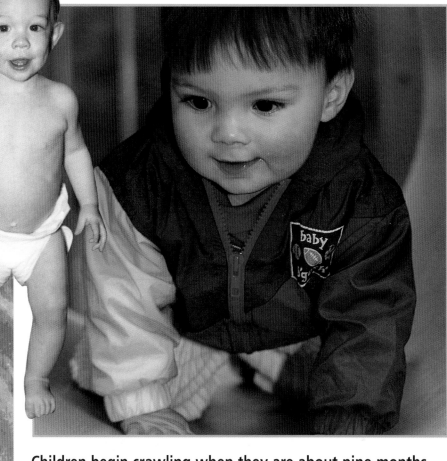

Children grow and learn quickly. As they grow, they gain more control over their bodies. They are able to do more for themselves. Babies can drink milk and juice. Young children can eat solid foods, but their parents must feed them. Older children can feed themselves.

Children begin crawling when they are about nine months old. They start walking on their own when they are about fifteen months old.

Humans learn by experience. They watch and listen to the world around them. They try new things. Babies must be watched carefully so they do not try something dangerous.

People grow two sets of teeth in their lifetime: **deciduous** (baby teeth) and permanent teeth.

Children keep growing until they are about ten – fourteen years old. After this time, children enter **adolescence**. Adolescence is the time when a child's body becomes more like an adult's. Humans usually finish growing by the time they are twenty years old. After that, humans may gain weight, but they do not grow taller.

As children reach adolescence, they become more and more independent.

Activity

Growth Chart

Make a growth chart for yourself. Ask your parents if you can make it on a wall or inside a closet door. Stand straight with your heels against the wall. Draw a short line with a pencil for your height. Label it with the date. Check your height and mark it again every six months.

Adulthood

Adults do not grow, but their bodies continue to change. Body cells are always being created and repaired. Many animals, some humans included, spend their adulthood having children and raising them.

Humans do not grow taller after they become adults, but astronauts measure taller in space without the force of **gravity** on their bodies. Astronauts measure at normal height when they return to Earth.

The body starts to wear out with age. The older a body becomes, the harder it is to fight off infections and disease. The body also begins to wrinkle and hair turns gray. Older people may even become shorter. The spaces between the bones in the **spine** shrink as people age.

The time an animal lives between its birth and death is called its lifespan. Many things affect how long an animal lives. Good food and healthy habits help people live longer.

The average lifespan for a human is sixty to seventy-five years. Exercise and healthy eating can help people live even longer.

Activity

Life Stages
Draw a picture of each of the following stages in the human lifespan.

- Adolescence
- Adulthood
- Infancy
- Childhood
- Old Age

Draw arrows between the stages to show them in order.

The lifespan of a wild elephant is similar to a human's. These elephants can live up to sixty-five years.

Broccoli for Breakfast?

No single food can give your body everything it needs. Even a healthy food such as broccoli is not enough if that is all you eat. Your body needs many different nutrients. Nutritionists take special classes to learn which foods the body needs to stay healthy. Nutritionists then help people choose the best foods to eat.

Nutritionists say people should eat at least one serving from each level of the food pyramid every day.

Fats, oils, and sweets

Milk, yogurt, cheese, meat, fish, eggs, poultry, beans, and nuts

Vegetables and fruit

Bread, cereal, grains, and pasta

Some nutritionists work in schools and teach children about healthy eating. Others plan meals for people who stay in hospitals. A nutritionist may even work with a sports coach to make sure athletes eat food that will give them more energy.

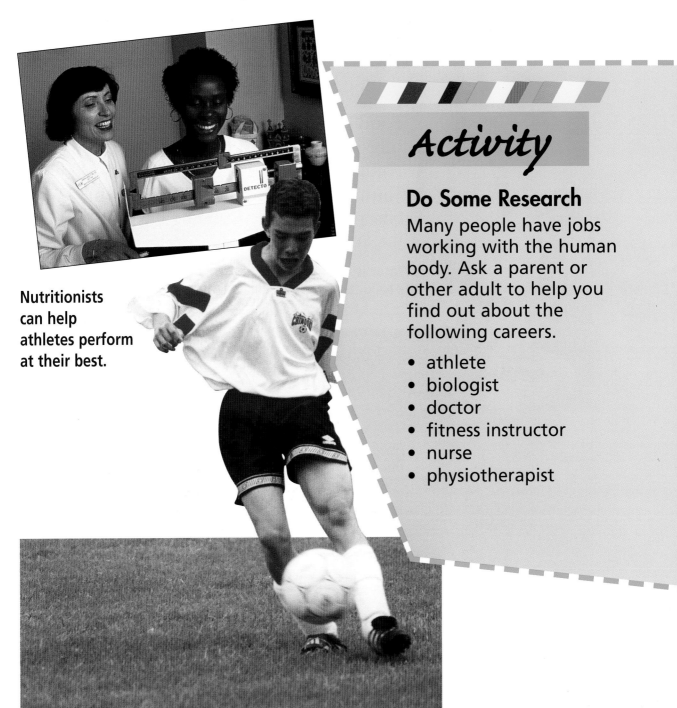

Nutritionists can help athletes perform at their best.

Activity

Do Some Research

Many people have jobs working with the human body. Ask a parent or other adult to help you find out about the following careers.

- athlete
- biologist
- doctor
- fitness instructor
- nurse
- physiotherapist

Healthy Bodies

The human body does many jobs. It senses the world around itself. It makes decisions. It moves, works, plays, and talks. It needs to be healthy to do these jobs well. To stay healthy, a human body needs food, water, exercise, and rest.

Food provides nutrients, or fuel. Your body needs nutrients to do work. When you feel hungry, your body is saying your energy and nutrients are running low. When you feel sleepy, your body is saying it is time for rest.

Water is the best thing to drink when the body is thirsty.

After exercise, the body often requires rest to give muscles time to recover.

Here are a few ways to keep your body in shape:

1. Get plenty of sleep. Most children need about twelve hours of sleep every day.
2. Eat healthy foods. The food pyramid on page 26 shows the major food groups the body needs to run well.
3. Get on your feet and exercise every day. Your muscles will thank you.
4. Wash your hands often. This will wash away germs on your skin that might make you sick.
5. Wear a hat and sunscreen lotion if you play outside in the sunshine. This will protect your skin from burning.

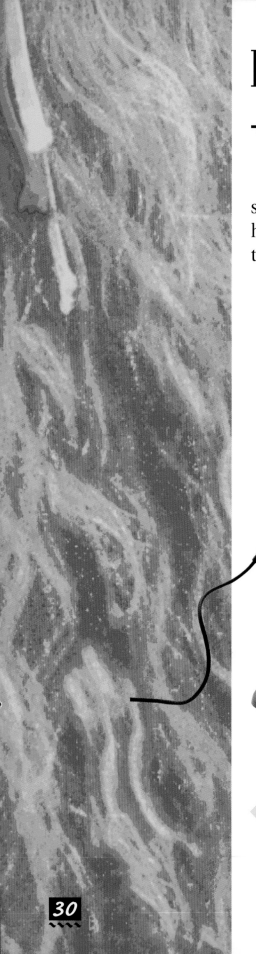

Beyond Our Bodies

We humans want to do many more things than our bodies let us do. People have made tools to help us see and hear farther, travel faster, and climb higher and lower. Which tool would you use to do the following?

Hear better

Climb HIGHER

Move after injury

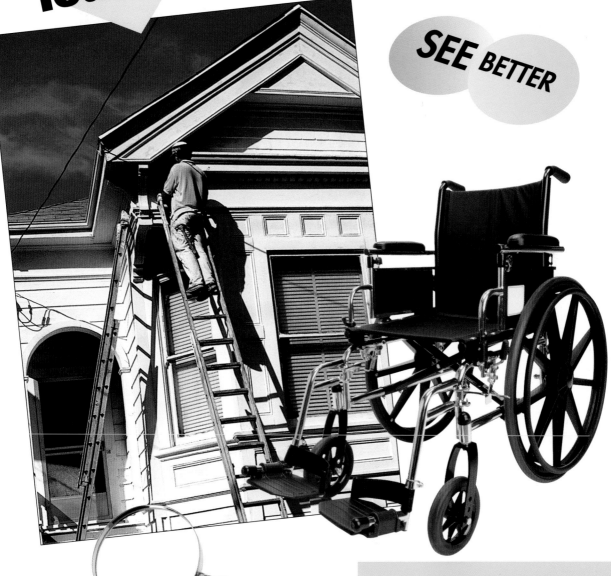

speak **louder**

SEE *BETTER*

GO FASTER

Answer:
Bicycle: Go faster
Magnifying glass: See better
Ladder: Climb higher
Microphone: Speak louder
Stethoscope: Hear better
Wheelchair: Move after injury

Glossary

adolescence: the stage when a child's body grows into adult form.

ancestors: the people from whom you are descended, including your parents, grandparents, great-grandparents, and so on.

bladder: a soft, thin bag in the body that holds liquid waste.

carbon dioxide: a colorless, odorless gas that you exhale when you breathe.

deciduous teeth: the first set of teeth, also called milk teeth.

gravity: a force that pulls objects downward, toward Earth.

intestines: the long tubes of the stomach where the last stages of digestion take place.

involuntary: done without thought or attention.

marrow: soft, fatty tissue in the center of bones.

nervous system: a system that connects the brain with the rest of the body.

nutrients: substances in food the body needs in order to stay healthy.

pregnancy: the condition in which a woman has a baby growing inside her.

rectum: the end of the intestines, which collects waste from food.

spine: the backbone needed for a person to sit and stand up.

streamlined: shaped to allow air and water to move past easily.

voluntary: (muscles) moved by a person's own will.

Index

Web Sites

faculty.washington.edu/chudler/neurok.html

www.surfnetkids.com/heart.htm

faculty.washington.edu/chudler/bbb.html

www.cellsalive.com

Some web sites stay current longer than others. For further web sites, use your search engines to locate the following topics: *circulation, fingerprints, nutrition,* and *teeth.*